DISASTERS IN HISTORY

THE CHALLENGER EXPLOSION

by Heather Adamson
illustrated by Brian Bascle

Consultant:

James Gerard

Aerospace Education Specialist

Kennedy Space Center

Capstone
press

Mankato, Minnesota

Graphic Library is published by Capstone Press,
151 Good Counsel Drive, P.O. Box 669, Mankato, Minnesota 56002.
www.capstonepress.com

1 2 3 4 5 6 11 10 09 08 07 06

Library of Congress Cataloging-in-Publication Data
Adamson, Heather, 1974–
    The Challenger explosion / by Heather Adamson; illustrated by Brian Bascle.
    p. cm.—(Graphic library. Disasters in history)
    Includes bibliographical references and index.
    ISBN-13: 978-0-7368-5478-8 (hardcover)
    ISBN-10: 0-7368-5478-9 (hardcover)
    1. Challenger (Spacecraft)—Accidents—Juvenile literature. 2. Space shuttles—Juvenile
literature. 3. McAuliffe, Christa, 1948-1986—Juvenile literature. 4. Astronauts—United States—
Juvenile literature. I. Bascle, Brian. II. Title. III. Series.
TL867.A33 2006
363.12'416—dc22   2005031234

Summary: In graphic novel format, tells the story of Christa McAuliffe and the six other NASA
astronauts who lost their lives in the Challenger space shuttle disaster on January 28, 1986.

Art Direction and Design
Jason Knudson

Storyboard Artist
Alison Thiele

Editor
Christopher Harbo

Editor's note: Direct quotations from primary sources are indicated by a yellow background.

Direct quotations appear on the following pages:
Page 5, from "Remarks of the Vice President Announcing the Winner of the Teacher in Space
    Project," 1985 (http://www.reagan.utexas.edu/archives/speeches/1985/71985a.htm).
Page 14, from *Report of the Presidential Commission on the Space Shuttle Challenger Accident*,
    1986 (http://history.nasa.gov/rogersrep/51lcover.htm).
Pages 18 (bottom, both), 19 (bottom), from "Transcript of the *Challenger* Crew Comments from
    the Operational Recorder.", 1986 (http://history.nasa.gov/transcript.htm).
Pages 18 (top), 22 from "Flight Director and NASA Select Audio Mix." *Spaceflight Now: The
    Challenger Accident*, 1986 (http://spaceflightnow.com/challenger/Video/loops_qt.html).
Page 27 (both), from "Explosion of the Space Shuttle *Challenger* Address to the Nation. January
    28, 1986." by President Ronald W. Reagan, 1986 (http://history.nasa.gov/reagan12886.html).

TABLE OF CONTENTS

CHAPTER 1

A TEACHER IN SPACE

In 1981, the United States launched its first space shuttle. For the first time, a spacecraft could be reused.

RUMBLE!

Soon, astronauts carried out several space shuttle missions each year. Some people believed space shuttles might one day carry regular citizens into space.

In 1984, President Ronald Reagan announced that NASA would send a teacher into space. He thought a teacher could explain what space travel was like to the public.

More than 11,000 teachers applied. On July 19, 1985, Vice President George H. W. Bush announced the winner from 10 finalists.

NASA has searched the Nation for a teacher with the right stuff. And the winner—

—Christa McAuliffe.

Christa was a high school social studies teacher from Concord, New Hampshire. She had to leave her job and her husband and children for five months of training in Houston, Texas.

We'll be watching for you in space!

WE'LL MISS YOU, MRS. McAULIFFE!

I'll be back in the classroom before you know it.

CHAPTER 2

MISSION 51L

Six other astronauts trained with Christa and Barbara for the shuttle mission. Mission commander Dick Scobee and shuttle pilot Michael Smith introduced Christa and Barbara to high speed flight in their T-38 jets.

Good afternoon, ladies.

This won't be your everyday airplane ride.

Yeah, let's see how teachers handle g-forces. Hope you brought your air sick bags!

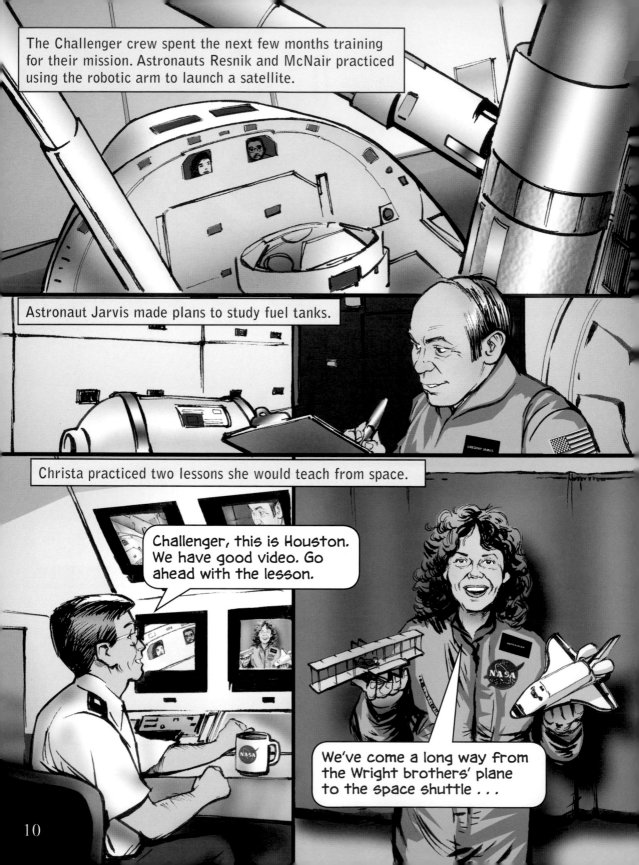

The Challenger crew spent the next few months training for their mission. Astronauts Resnik and McNair practiced using the robotic arm to launch a satellite.

Astronaut Jarvis made plans to study fuel tanks.

Christa practiced two lessons she would teach from space.

Challenger, this is Houston. We have good video. Go ahead with the lesson.

We've come a long way from the Wright brothers' plane to the space shuttle . . .

On January 27, 1986, the crew sat down to a prelaunch breakfast. The shuttle launch was originally scheduled for January 22. It had been delayed five times in the last few days.

Looks like we're finally going today—you ready?

No teacher's ever been more ready to give two lessons.

Good morning, Bob.

Good Luck!

Bye!

Good morning. Just sit tight and I'll get you strapped in.

CHAPTER 3

LIFT OFF TO DISASTER

On the morning of January 28, 1986, crowds gathered again in the cold to watch the launch.

I can't believe our daughter is going into space.

Look at all the ice!

Don't worry, they won't launch if it isn't safe.

Oh, my!

Noooo!

Soon after the disaster, the families of the astronauts gathered at Kennedy Space Center.

Why?! Why did this happen?

CHAPTER 4

THE WORLD MOURNS

People across the country had been watching this flight. They were saddened when the *Challenger* astronauts were lost.

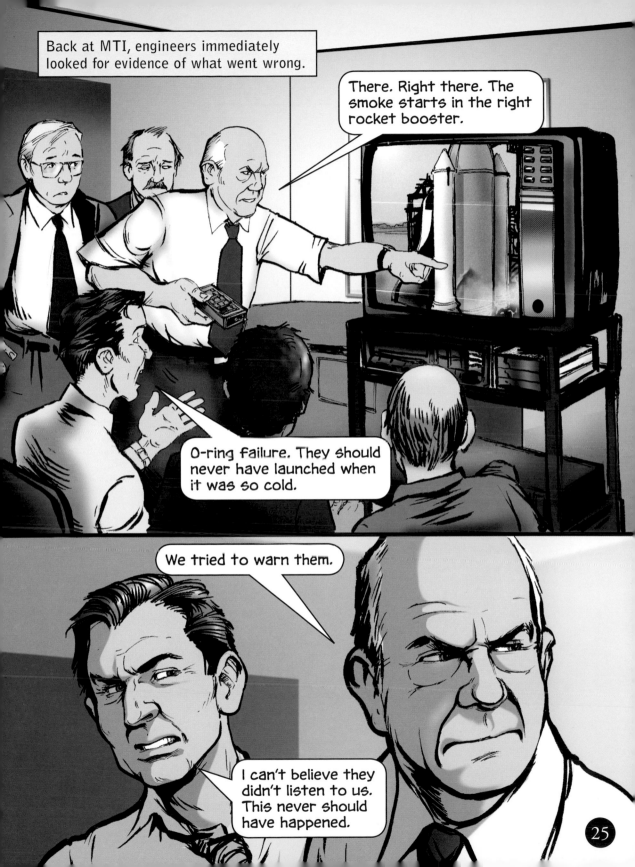

President Ronald Reagan was supposed to give a State of the Union address the evening of January 28. Instead, he spoke to the nation about the *Challenger* explosion.

Tonight we mourn seven heroes.

We've grown used to the idea of space, and perhaps we forget that we've only just begun. We're still pioneers.

It's all part of taking a chance and expanding man's horizons. The Challenger crew was pulling us into the future, and we'll continue to follow them.

After the *Challenger* disaster, NASA grounded the shuttle program for more than two years. The three remaining shuttles were upgraded with many new safety features. Finally, in September 1988, the shuttle *Discovery* launched safely and returned the United States to space.

Scobee

Smith

Resnik

McNair

Onizuka

Jarvis

McAuliffe

MORE ABOUT THE CHALLENGER EXPLOSION

⭐ *Challenger* reached an altitude of more than 9 miles above the earth before it exploded over the ocean.

⭐ A commission report determined that O-ring failure was the cause of *Challenger*'s explosion. Cold weather was noted as a factor in the O-ring failure.

⭐ Only about 50 percent of the shuttle was recovered before the search for debris was called off. Every once in awhile, pieces are still discovered. Two large sections washed ashore in Cocoa Beach, Florida, 10 years after the accident.

⭐ Barbara Morgan continued working with the Teacher in Space program after the *Challenger* accident. In January 1998, NASA selected her to be the first Educator Astronaut. She went through full astronaut training. Morgan is assigned to the crew of STS-118.

⭐ The families of the *Challenger* astronauts worked together to create Challenger Centers. These educational centers around the country let students learn about space and teamwork by simulating space missions.

★ The fleet of space shuttles was grounded for more than two years after *Challenger*'s explosion. New safety features were added to the shuttle and engineers developed better seals for the rocket boosters.

★ Many memorials for *Challenger* and its crew can be found around the world. People stroll through Challenger Seven Memorial Park in Texas. A monument marks where crew remains are buried in Arlington National Cemetery.

★ President Reagan read part of the poem, "High Flight" by John Gillespie Magee Jr. in his speech about *Challenger*. The poem is often a favorite of astronauts and pilots. It was a favorite of Christa McAuliffe and read at her memorial service.

GLOSSARY

engineer (en-juh-NIHR)—a person who is trained to design and build machines

executive (eg-ZEK-yuh-tiv)—someone who has a senior job in a company and is involved in planning the future

g-force (JEE-forss)—the force of gravity or acceleration on a body

malfunction (mal-FUHNGK-shuhn)—to fail to operate normally

O-ring (OH-ring)—a rubber ring that seals the joints in solid rocket boosters

pioneer (pye-uh-NEER)—someone who explores an unknown territory or settles there

INTERNET SITES

FactHound offers a safe, fun way to find Internet sites related to this book. All of the sites on FactHound have been researched by our staff.

Here's how:

1. *Visit www.facthound.com*
2. Type in this special code **0736854789** for age-appropriate sites. Or enter a search word related to this book for a more general search.
3. Click on the **Fetch It** button.

FactHound will fetch the best sites for you!

READ MORE

Holden, Henry M. *The Tragedy of the Space Shuttle Challenger.* Space Flight Adventures and Disasters. Berkeley Heights, N.J.: MyReportLinks.com Books, 2004.

McNeese, Tim. *The Challenger Disaster.* Cornerstones of Freedom. New York: Children's Press, 2003.

Stille, Darlene R. *Space Shuttle.* Transportation. Minneapolis, Minn.: Compass Point Books, 2004.

Streissguth, Thomas. *The Challenger: The Explosion on Liftoff.* Disaster! Mankato, Minn.: Capstone High-Interest Books, 2003.

BIBLIOGRAPHY

Corrigan, Grace George. *A Journal for Christa.* Lincoln: University of Nebraska Press, 1993.

Hohler, Robert T. *I Touch the Future . . . the Story of Christa McAuliffe.* New York: Random House, 1986.

Lewis, Richard S. *Challenger: The Final Voyage.* New York: Columbia University Press, 1988.

NASA History Office. *Report of the Presidential Commission on the Space Shuttle Challenger Accident.* http://history.nasa.gov/rogersrep/51lcover.htm.

INDEX